THE MOST INFLUENTIAL
WOMEN
IN POLITICS

BREAKING THE GLASS CEILING
THE MOST INFLUENTIAL WOMEN™

THE MOST INFLUENTIAL
WOMEN
IN POLITICS

RAJDEEP PAULUS

Rosen
YA
New York

Published in 2019 by The Rosen Publishing Group, Inc.
29 East 21st Street, New York, NY 10010

Library of Congress Cataloging-in-Publication Data

Names: Paulus, Rajdeep, author.
Title: The most influential women in politics / Rajdeep Paulus.
Description: New York : Rosen Publishing, 2019. | Series: Breaking the glass ceiling : the most influential women | Includes bibliographical references and index. | Audience: Grades 7–12.
Identifiers: LCCN 2017055425| ISBN 9781508179689 (library bound) | ISBN 9781508179832 (pbk.)
Subjects: LCSH: Women politicians—Biography—Juvenile literature. | Women heads of state—Biography—Juvenile literature. | Women—Political activity—Juvenile literature.
Classification: LCC HQ1236 .P376 2019 | DDC 320.082—dc23
LC record available at https://lccn.loc.gov/2017055425

Manufactured in the United States of America

On the cover: As the first African American First Lady, Michelle Obama was far more than the president's fashionable wife. She supported military families and encouraged healthy eating, especially for kids.

CONTENTS

Throughout history, women have shaped world politics, but they often met with resistance. Opportunities for women to raise their voices and become instruments of change developed slowly, and each woman who stepped forward against great odds paved the way for all the women who dare to dream political dreams. Some women who objected to the status quo never reached their goals but pressed on with conviction, perseverance, and sacrifice.

Suffrage, or the right to vote, has been a major political battleground for women around the world. Many countries passed laws allowing women to vote throughout the twentieth century: several in the years following World War I, including Canada and the United States, and many more after the end of World War II in 1945. In the United States, because some states passed laws regarding women's political rights long before the nation as a whole did, the first woman served in Congress before women nationwide gained the right to vote in 1920. Jeannette Rankin of Montana was elected to Congress in 1916.

Although many countries simultaneously granted women the right to be elected and to vote, in some countries, women's right to run for office came long after their right

In 1916, Jeanette Rankin made history by becoming the first woman elected to the US Congress. She was also the only member of Congress to vote against the United States entering both World Wars.

to vote. Women in Saudi Arabia voted for the first time in a municipal election in 2015 and only gained the right to drive in 2017. Women's voting rights can be unstable. In Afghanistan, for example, the Taliban-controlled government revoked women's voting rights in the country when it ruled from 1996 to 2001.

Despite ongoing trials, women have risen to positions of political leadership. The history of international female leaders includes congresswomen, governors, mayors, prime ministers, presidents, and queens. This book explores the lives and accomplishments of female political figures from around the world, such as Hillary Clinton, Queen Elizabeth II, Indira Gandhi, Nikki Haley, Condoleezza Rice, and Ellen Johnson Sirleaf. Many of these accomplished individuals were the first women to attain such prominent positions in their countries. The journey is far from over as women strive to lead countries and governments toward diversity, equality, and justice.

CHAPTER ONE

QUEENS, REGENTS, AND ROYALTY

W omen bearing titles of royalty usually inherited their crowns, but not always. Some married into royal families, and others attained their positions after political uprisings and changes in power. Some ruled on the sidelines in the shadow of the king. Bearing titles such as queen, princess, empress, and pharaoh, women are remembered for more than their portraits or wealth. They used their power and influence to make their marks in history.

Hatshepsut

Hatshepsut ruled Egypt from 1479 until 1458 BCE and is famous for presenting herself as a male king during her reign, sporting a king's kilt and fake, pharaohlike beard. When her husband and half

Hatshepsut reigned over Egypt from 1479 until 1458 BCE. Centuries later, in 1899, her tomb was discovered by British archaeologist Howard Carter.

brother, Thutmose II, passed away in 1479 BCE, the throne passed to his son, Thutmose III (son of her husband and a harem wife). Thutmose III was too young to rule, so Hatshepsut ruled as regent until he came of age. However, in 1473, Hatshepsut took matters into her own hands and assumed the full title and power of a pharaoh, joining Thutmose III as coruler. To display her success, Hatshepsut erected one hundred foot (thirty-meter)–tall monuments and built up the infrastructure of Egypt with new roads and sanctuaries.

Hatshepsut's temple displayed hundreds of larger-than-life statues of herself. The temple was masculine in nature and recognizable from far away. It was known for its pools and gardens, as opposed to the fortress-like monuments of her predecessors. When Thutmose III was old enough to rule, Hatshepsut handed over the throne peacefully. Two decades later, however, he attempted to erase every trace of Hatshepsut. The statues and monuments built during her rule were destroyed or defaced.

Cleopatra VII

Cleopatra VII was queen of Egypt from 51 BCE until 30 BCE. Following the death of her father, Cleopatra became coheir of Egypt with her brother, Ptolemy XIII. It is likely, though not proven, that they married, which would have been in accordance with Egyptian custom.

Perhaps the sibling factor contributes to historians' conclusions that this queen did not want

Cleopatra VII's rule marked the end of pharaohs ruling over Egypt. Here she is depicted meeting her last husband, Mark Antony, the man she chose to be buried with.

to share the throne. Known for her ruthless ascent to power, the last pharaoh of Egypt overthrew her siblings with the help of Roman generals Julius Caesar and Mark Antony in order to secure her position. With her siblings either killed in battle or murdered, Cleopatra brought a season of peace to Egypt after many years of civil war. History paints her as a popular leader, crediting her for Egypt's thriving economy and independence from Roman rule.

Cleopatra's ethnicity is not known, but she studied the Egyptian language and even had portraits of herself commissioned in the traditional Egyptian style for the time. She was applauded for her patriotism and savvy foreign policies. She brought prosperity to the Egyptian economy while asserting her independence from the Roman Empire. The ongoing struggle between empires came to a head after Caesar's death. On August 12, 30 BCE, at the age of thirty-nine, she followed her last husband, Mark Antony, and committed suicide. The two were buried together in a single tomb.

Boudicca

Boudicca, the widow of King Prasutagus of the British Celtic Iceni tribe, was one of the rare queens who went to the front lines herself instead of simply sending their military forces into battle for her. Boudicca led a revolution against Roman rule in 60 CE, after Roman troops defiled, pillaged, and destroyed Icenian people, property, and land. Twenty years of Roman occupation came to a violent crossroads, and Boudicca, queen of Iceni, was at the head of the rebellion. Her revolt began with several victories when she led her troops against the cities of Colchester, London, and St. Albans. Joined by other tribes also fed up with Roman occupation and mistreatment, the British chariots charged Roman soldiers, but their momentary victory was met with a shower of arrows that pierced their unprotected bodies.

Even the retreat was met with defeat, as the bodies of dead humans and animals deterred the wagons. According to Elizabeth Norton's 2015 story, "Women Rule," in *Britain* magazine, it was a massacre, and Boudicca is said to have poisoned herself, joining the almost eighty thousand British people who died in the rebellion. The Romans claimed four hundred of their own soldiers were lost in the battle. Boudicca is remembered for fighting for her daughters and her people, as well as for standing up in the face of insurmountable odds. Her example inspired subsequent efforts to free Britain from Roman rule.

Galla Placidia

Galla Placidia, the daughter of the Roman emperor Theodosius I, was born around 390 CE. She became the regent to her son, the Roman emperor Valentinian III, after the death of her brother Honorius, and her second husband. She survived being taken hostage by the Visigoths, or Goths. She was mistreated and was forced to marry Ataulf, the leader of the Goths. Placidia returned to her family after Ataulf's death in Barcelona, Spain. In 417, she married the Roman general Constantius, and her brother Honorius ruled the Western Roman Empire. The siblings parted ways after a disagreement and Galla fled to the courts of Theodosius II. After her brother Honorius's death and her son's coronation, Placidia returned to rule until her son was old enough to take over the throne.

When the Roman Empire embraced Christianity, Placidia spent countless royal dollars building churches and cathedrals with early Byzantine mosaics. Her role as regent when her young son was crowned emperor over Rome and its provinces gave her the power to shape the empire before its eventual decline. Placidia ruled in a time when it was uncommon for women to take on roles of leadership and authority. During her twelve-year position as regent, the Roman army withstood countless invasions. These were the last of Rome's glory days.

Catherine the Great

Catherine the Great was born on April 21, 1729, a German princess whose fairytale-like journey began when Empress Elizabeth of Russia asked her to visit when she was fifteen years old. After meeting the Grand Duke Peter, converting to the Russian Orthodox faith, and changing her name from Sophie to Catherine, she married Peter a year later. The fairy tale didn't last long, and after Empress Elizabeth died in 1761, Peter III was the rightful heir. He made enemies quickly, and Catherine, alongside her lover Grigory Orlov, rallied an army in St. Petersburg and overthrew Peter. She declared herself the ruler of Russia and was crowned empress in Moscow. Peter was assassinated while in the custody of his captors, in the village of Ropsha.

Catherine's rule was marked with many domestic and foreign accomplishments. Her victorious first war against the Ottoman Empire between 1768 and 1774 resulted in Russia becoming the strongest force in the Middle East. As czar, Catherine dealt with domestic opposition, particularly from the rebel peasant leader the Cossack Yemelyan Pugachev and his tens of thousands of followers. Some accounts suggest that Pugachev claimed to be her dead husband, Peter. After several major battles, Pugachev was overthrown and peace was restored in Russia.

Off the battlefields on the domestic front, Catherine brought notable development of the arts, literature, and natural sciences in Russian society. Catherine's accomplishments included both judiciary and education reforms. She proposed to reshape the outdated laws of 1649 with "The Instruction," a system that provided equal protection for all citizens and focused on prevention rather than punishment of crime. These changes never took a lasting hold

In this 1875 copy of a 1762 portrait by V. Eriksen, Catherine the Great poses with boots, hat, and sword on her decorated horse.

with her government or the people. Her education reforms were more successful. She created many new schools before her death.

The downside of her laws was that they benefited the noble class, known as the intelligentsia, and left the common citizens and serfs with little aid. This did little to address Russia's poverty and its inability to keep up with the rapidly developing economies of Germany, Japan, and America. Catherine feared her throne would be taken over by a rival family member—particularly her mentally unstable son Paul I—so she proposed to change the laws regarding inheritance of leadership. The new laws would have given her grandson Alexander a shot at the crown, but she passed away on November 6, 1796, and Paul destroyed all of Catherine's documents regarding succession laws that he could find.

Queen Elizabeth II

As queen since 1952, Elizabeth II has reigned over the United Kingdom of Great Britain and Northern Ireland longer than any other monarch. Famous for much more than her royal wave, Elizabeth II was born in 1926 in Mayfair, London. Her father became King George VI when his brother Edward VIII abdicated in 1936. England celebrated her Sapphire Jubilee, commemorating sixty-five years of service in 2017. The queen wore a sapphire dress with sapphire jewelry and a sapphire-studded crown for her portrait.

THE TREATY OF KUCHUK KAINARJI

Catherine the Great's rule of Russia was marked by the Russo-Turkish Wars. When Russia won the first of these wars, Catherine II and Sultan Mustafa III of the Ottoman Empire and Turkey signed a peace treaty called the Treaty of Kuchuk Kainarji. The Treaty of Kuchuk Kainarji allowed Russia to centralize its powers even more, granting Russia more power over the surrounding lands. The treaty gave Kerch and other Black Sea ports in the Crimea to Russia and declared the rest of Crimea independent. Russian trading ships gained permission to pass through Turkish waters unharmed. Russia also gained rights on behalf of the Greek Orthodox minority living under the Sultan, protecting them from religious persecution. The Treaty of Kuchuk Kainarji laid the foundation for Crimea becoming a full part of Russia in 1783. It marked the beginning of Russia's tenure as a force to be reckoned with in continental Europe under Catherine the Great.

As the figurehead of the United Kingdom and the Commonwealth for such a long time, Queen Elizabeth has been a voice for change in society, at home and abroad, particularly through her more than six hundred charities, many of which fund youth

Queen Elizabeth attends a service held in St. Paul's Cathedral for the order of the British Empire in 2012.

programs and environmental protection projects. With the expansion of democracy, the queen's role has changed. Today, she is more of a figurehead than an authority. But one thing never changed: she is held in high regard all over the world. Over the years, the queen has welcomed countless world leaders, visited schools, and attended fundraisers. She was supportive of the decision in 2011 to allow the first-born child to be first in the line of succession regardless of gender. Previously, male heirs had taken precedence. For example, if Elizabeth had had a younger brother, he would have been king even though she was older.

Queen Elizabeth and her husband, Prince Philip, celebrated seventy years of marriage on November 20, 2017. She has relished her roles as mother, grandmother, and great-grandmother. She is no stranger to loss and sorrow, however. Queen Elizabeth lived through the deaths of her mother, sister, and former daughter-in-law, Princess Diana. She has addressed the public after several terrorist attacks. Elizabeth II expressed her grief for the victims and their families after the Manchester attack at an Ariana Grande concert in 2017. She also applauded the first responders and the citizens who worked to help each other in the midst of chaos and fear, calling for reexamining the antiterrorist strategies of the United Kingdom. In 2018, she is in her nineties, but she continues to speak up with authority and grace.

Princess Diana

Princess Diana of England was born on July 1, 1961. She married Prince Charles, Queen Elizabeth's first-born son on July 29, 1981, when she was twenty years old and he was thirty-two. Diana was an exceptional princess. In April 1987, during the AIDS crisis, when homophobia was on the rise, Diana shook hands without gloves with a man suffering from AIDS at London's Middlesex Hospital, helping to dispel the myth that AIDS was contagious from a simple touch. In 1997, Diana walked through an African minefield, responding to the Red Cross's cry to ban landmines in the war-torn country of Angola. Diana shed light on issues such as bulimia, depression, and self-harm. She met revolutionary leader and freedom fighter Nelson Mandela in 1997 to discuss AIDS in South Africa.

Diana's formal title of Her Royal Highness was removed following her divorce from Prince Charles after fifteen years of marriage in 1996, and her title became simply Diana, Princess of Wales. She will always be remembered as Princess Diana. Diana's life ended in a car wreck in Paris on August 31, 1997, when she was thirty-six years old. Tens of thousands of her admirers around the world grieved her death, gathering at her funeral at Westminster Abbey and watching the event on television.

Princess Diana used her position as a member of the royal family of England to bring attention to mental and public health issues such as AIDS, eating disorders, and depression.

Queen Rania Al Abdullah

Queen Rania of Jordan worked in banking and information technology after studying business in college. Her marriage to Prince Abdullah bin Al Hussein in 1993 was followed by the birth of their four children. Queen Rania advocates for women and children, tirelessly petitioning for their access to education and equal opportunity. Her stand for education earned her global recognition, and she's been named honorary chair of the United Nations Girls' Education Initiative.

In addition to helping youth, Queen Rania has helped countless women jump-start their businesses through programs that offer small starter loans. Her activism has earned her many honors and awards, and she continues to use her success to expand her reach, founding both

Queen Rania of Jordan plays with young Rohingya Muslim refugees on a visit to the Kutupalong refugee camp in Ukhia, Bangladesh, on October 23, 2017.

the Jordan Education Initiative and Queen Rania Teacher Academy, working in collaboration with her country's Ministry of Education. Appealing to today's generation, Queen Rania launched a vlog in March 2008 in which her primary goal was to dispel stereotypes associated with the Arab world. In 2017, she met refugees who had fled to Bangladesh and spoke up about the atrocities against the Rohingya Muslims of Myanmar, urging a global response to the ethnic cleansing that was occurring. Queen Rania is also a children's book author. Her book *The Sandwich Swap* reflects her own childhood experiences.

CHAPTER TWO

MS. PRIME MINISTER AT YOUR SERVICE

To become a prime minister, an official is selected by his or her party as the party leader, and if the party wins a majority in any given election, the party leader becomes the parliament's prime minister. If a particular party goes on to keep the majority for any given number of years, the prime minister continues to lead with that title unless he or she chooses to step down or resign, which has happened in the United Kingdom over notable disagreements and political pressure from within and outside the party.

A prime minister is the head of the cabinet and can introduce new laws to be voted on, but he or she is ultimately accountable to the country or kingdom's figurehead, usually a king or queen, as is the case in the United Kingdom. The prime minister's primary roles also include meeting with foreign officials and representing the country as the key leader under the royal head. Both the presidents and prime ministers appoint key members to federal agencies and the cabinet.

Prime ministers of various countries have often governed in countries where women were treated as second-class citizens and didn't have the same rights as men.

Indira Gandhi

Indira Gandhi was born on November 19, 1917, and grew up in the years just before India's birth as a country. Her father, Jawaharlal Nehru, became the first prime minister of India right after the country achieved independence in 1947. Indira Gandhi was elected to the mainly honorary role of president of her father's Congress Party in 1959 and later served as minister of information and broadcasting under Prime Minister Lal Bahadur Shastri, who held the office after Nehru passed away in 1964. When Shastri passed away in 1966, Gandhi was named leader of the Congress Party.

Indira Gandhi enjoys a ride around London after her father, Jawaharlal Nehru, received the Freedom of the City honor from the British government.

When the Congress Party won the 1967 elections, Gandhi became the first female prime minister of India. She served four nonconsecutive terms as prime minister between 1966 and 1984. Under Gandhi's leadership, India defeated Pakistan in a war that led to the creation of the newly independent country of Bangladesh in 1971. While Prime Minister Gandhi helped bolster India's self-sustainability with agricultural reforms, she also declared a state of emergency in 1975 when she was accused of election corruption, arresting many members of her opposing party without trial, limiting civil liberties, and censoring the press for two years.

Prime Minister Gandhi knew how to play both sides of the fence. She visited US president Lyndon Johnson to ask for aid for her poverty-stricken citizens and then turned around and sided with the Soviet Union and condemned America for its invasion of Vietnam.

Listening to the advice of her son Sanjay, the prime minister executed two policies that hurt India. Forced sterilization pushed an inhumane method of population control on the poorest of India's citizens, and a slum demolition program left many Indians homeless when their shelters were destroyed. In an attempt to quash a rebellion by a small faction of militant Sikhs in 1984, Prime Minister Gandhi authorized an invasion of the Golden Temple, the most sacred place for Sikhs. This resulted in the deaths of hundreds of innocent citizens, sparked

THE TRIALS OF INDIRA GANDHI

While India's independence from Britain in 1947 was a major step forward, it didn't erase the internal religious divisions that caused ongoing civil disputes in the new democracy. Indira Gandhi was no stranger to this turmoil. A woman who enjoyed both seasons of extreme popularity and overwhelming resistance in her political life, Prime Minister Indira Gandhi's personal life was marked by rebellion and tragedy. For example, she married a man outside her family's religion, which was frowned upon in Indian culture. She suffered the loss of her second-born son, Sanjay, who died in a plane crash in 1980. She was imprisoned twice, once for speaking out against British rule before independence and once for corruption allegations during her years as prime minister. Her assassination brought a violent end to the troubled days of India's first female prime minister.

international outrage, and ultimately led to her assassination four months later by two of her own Sikh bodyguards. Rajiv, her only son still alive, became the next prime minister.

Golda Meir

Golda Meir was born on May 3, 1898, in the Ukraine, but her Jewish heritage led her to the Middle East in 1921. Meir's early years as a political activist earned her an invitation to be part of the twenty-five signatures on Israel's Declaration of Independence on May 14, 1948. Before Israel's independence, Meir had her hand in many political affairs, both domestic and foreign, raising awareness and support for Palestinian Jews who lacked jobs, land, housing, and medical care.

Between 1949 and 1966, Meir served as the minister of labor and later foreign minister of Israel. Her years as an ambassador to the Soviet

Former Israeli prime minister Golda Meir approached military action cautiously, saying, "There's no difference between one's killing and making decisions that will send others to kill. It's exactly the same thing, or even worse."

Union granted her experience and connections. In 1966, she became the secretary-general of the Mapai Party. She later held the same position in the Labor Party. In 1969, Meir was elected as the first female prime minister of Israel, and she started her governing years by helping to boost Israel's economy.

Meir's leadership took a nosedive in 1973. Tragedy broke out during Yom Kippur when Egyptian and Syrian troops attacked Israel on the Jewish Holy Day. This resulted in a bloodbath of more than 2,500 Israeli soldiers. Unable to accept her failure to react in time, Meir resigned as prime minister in 1974. Losing her battle with cancer, Meir died on December 8, 1978.

Sonia Gandhi

Sonia Gandhi, daughter-in-law of Indira Gandhi and wife of Prime Minister Rajiv Gandhi, was born into a Roman Catholic Italian family and met Rajiv in 1965 while they were both studying in Cambridge, England. They married in 1968, and she became a naturalized Indian citizen in 1983. In 1991, Prime Minister Gandhi, like his mother before him, was assassinated, leaving Sonia a widow. Sonia Gandhi wrote two books, one about her late husband, Rajiv, paying tribute to all his accomplishments as prime minister. The second was a book of letters between Indira Gandhi and her father, the first prime minister of independent India.

Sonia Gandhi was elected president of India's National Congress Party in 1998. In 1999, Gandhi was elected to parliament and in 2004, her party won the election, making her the first female foreign-born prime minister of India. Fearing the country's division over her not being of Indian descent, Gandhi deferred her position to the finance minister. Dr. Manmohan Singh became the new prime minister of India in her place one day before Gandhi's scheduled inauguration in 2004, a difficult decision she will always be remembered for making.

Benazir Bhutto

Benazir Bhutto was born on June 21, 1953, in Karachi, Pakistan. She was the daughter of Zulfikar Ali Bhutto, the founder and president of the Pakistan People's Party. Zulfikar was elected prime minister of Pakistan in 1973. Like Indira Gandhi of India, Benazir Bhutto studied at Oxford University in England, and her father brought her up with her future in politics in mind. Bhutto's father died at the hands of opposing military forces. She became the leader of the PPP, and Bhutto was placed under house arrest frequently between 1979 and 1984 by the military dictator General Muhammad Zia-ul-Haq. The loss of her father and her freedom would have made the average person quit, but Bhutto's story does not end there. General Zia and many of his party were killed in a plane crash in 1988. This gave Bhutto the opportunity to run for prime minister.

Benazir Bhutto poses by the ballot box on November 16, 1988, not long after she was freed from house arrest.

Bhutto became prime minister on December 1, 1988. She spent two terms combating accusations of bribery, corruption, and money laundering. Her verbal promises to restore Pakistan to a true democracy, to fight for women's rights, and to inaugurate a more open society were cut short with her removal from power, arrest, and self-imposed exile in England and Dubai in the late nineties.

Bhutto was officially pardoned by the government of Pakistan in 2007. She returned to her country and began to campaign for the next elections. However, resentment over her past ran strong in Pakistan, and her life was threatened during her campaign. Bhutto, along with several of her party members, was assassinated on December 27, 2007.

Yingluck Shinawatra

Yingluck Shinawatra was born on June 21, 1967, and grew up in one of Thailand's wealthiest households. Before entering politics, Yingluck held several executive positions in her family's business operations. In 2009, she was regarded as a possible political successor to her brother, Thaksin, a former prime minister who was ousted in a military coup in 2006. A self-exiled billionaire, Thaksin supported his sister's rise to power, and in May 2011, she became the head of the Phuea Thai Party. When the Phuea Thai Party won the majority in Thailand's 2011 election, Yingluck became the country's first female

Yingluck Shinawatra lost her position as prime minister and the confidence of Thai citizens because of a misguided scheme to falsely inflate the price of rice.

prime minister. In 2013, Yingluck gained the additional title of minister of defense.

Yingluck was forced to resign in 2014 after being convicted of an abuse of power. After being removed from office, the new government proceeded to officially impeach Yingluck in 2015, banning her from office for a minimum of five years. Yingluck and her party were accused of ignoring the corruption in a rice-subsidization program that resulted in huge quantities of rice being piled up in government facilities. Yingluck hoped to drive the price of rice up, which would benefit Thailand's rice farmers, who earn significantly less than other rice farmers around the word. Instead, the secret plan led to billions in financial losses, and Thailand lost its position as the top rice exporter. Yingluck followed in her brother's footsteps by exiling herself to avoid paying enormous fines and serving a ten-year prison sentence.

Margaret Thatcher

Margaret Thatcher (née Roberts) was born on October 13, 1925. Her father, Alfred Roberts, was a councilor in his local government. Like many daughters with political fathers, Thatcher was inspired by her father's political activities, often attending meetings with him. When she ran for government office for the first time, Thatcher lost the vote. Several failed campaigns later, she returned to Oxford to study Law. She won her first seat in Parliament in the election of 1959.

In May 1979, Thatcher led the Conservative Party to victory and became the first female prime minister of the United Kingdom. She governed for three terms and was responsible for establishing a national educational curriculum and amending the National Health Service.

During her years as prime minister, a crisis broke out between the Falkland Islands (a British territory) and Argentina, and an attack on British troops led to retaliations when negotiations didn't work. Thatcher earned praise for her handling of the conflict, and the victory gave the economically hurting nation of Britain a moment of hope and celebration.

BREXIT

"Brexit" is the term used to describe Britain's decision to exit the European Union, which won a majority of the vote in a referendum in 2016. Theresa May, the second female prime minister of the United Kingdom, and the Conservative Party (also called the Tories) lost its majority in the Parliament in the 2017 elections, leaving Prime Minister May at a disadvantage, especially on the issue of Brexit. The process of leaving the European Union is complex, and as of early 2018 Britain has not yet "Brexited." Many people in Britain believe this will be the first step to restoring Britain's economic independence and strength. Many others, however, think the decision to leave was a serious mistake. Prime Minister May opposed Brexit at first, but she's since changed her position and proposed that Brexit be carried out in 2021.

Thatcher held her position at the tail end of the Cold War. Although the primary conflict was between the United States and the Soviet Union, the allies on each side were clear, and the United Kingdom sided with the United States. Margaret Thatcher was a strong ally and friend of US president Ronald Reagan. Despite all of her accomplishments Thatcher is usually remembered

Aung San Suu Kyi is surrounded by her fellow citizens while speaking at a rally on October 22, 2015, the year her party, the National League for Democracy, won the election.

for her nickname, the Iron Lady, bestowed on her because she never shied away from expressing her disapproval of the Soviet Union and its policies, while maintaining a respectful relationship with Soviet leader Mikhail Gorbachev. Thatcher took the nickname as a compliment.

Aung San Suu Kyi

Aung San Suu Kyi was born in 1945 in Burma (now called Myanmar). Yet another daughter of an assassinated parent, her father, General Aung San, laid the foundation for her political ambitions. A graduate of Oxford University, Suu Kyi cofounded and became the leader of the National League for Democracy in 1988, and her party won the majority of seats in the 1990 election. Her desire for political freedom and her outspoken criticism of the military leaders of Myanmar who placed her under house arrest in 1989 made her a national symbol. She was awarded the 1990 Sakharov Prize from the European Parliament and the 1991 Nobel Peace Prize for her commitment to nonviolence during her struggle.

Although the National League for Democracy won 80 percent of the seats in the 1990 elections for parliament, the military refused to acknowledge its win. This threw the country into a state of unrest until 1995, when Suu Kyi was released. However, the military amended the constitution, restricting Suu Kyi from running for the head of the country or her political party.

Suu Kyi was subject to further instances of house arrest or detainment between 2000 and 2010, and her party dissolved under the military's opposition. The National League for Democracy did not emerge again until 2012, under President Thein Sein, and Suu Kyi announced her candidacy in the 2012 elections for parliament. Her party secured slightly more than forty seats in 2012, but in the 2015 elections, the National League for Democracy won majorities in both houses of parliament. Htin Kyaw, a close confidant of Suu Kyi, became president. The constitutional ban on Suu Kyi serving as president required the government to grant Suu Kyi a new title in order to serve in the government formally. In fact, they gave her two: foreign minister and state counselor, together granting her a governing role similar to that of a prime minister.

But the strife and struggle are far from over for Suu Kyi and her government as, in 2018, the world's eyes were on reports of severely unjust treatment of a minority group in Myanmar. Muslim Rohingyas have been forced to leave their homes by the hundreds of thousands, and the military-backed government led by the newly elected President Htin Kyaw and Suu Kyi were being questioned for the atrocities reported in what appears to be a strategic ethnic cleansing of the Rohingyas.

Angela Merkel

Angela Merkel was born in 1954 and grew up in East Germany. She studied to be a physicist and researched quantum chemistry at East Berlin's Academy of Sciences before she entered the world of politics.

In 1989, she joined the conservative Christian Democratic Union and was elected to Parliament in 1990. A student of Chancellor Helmut Kohl, she served under him as minister for women and youth and federal minister for the environment, nature conservation, and nuclear safety between 1991 and 1998. Kohl lost the election in 1998, but Merkel went on to become the secretary-general of the Christian Democratic Union and was elected party leader in 2000.

In 2005, Merkel's party won the election, and she became chancellor of Germany. She is the first woman to accomplish this. Merkel remained chancellor after two subsequent elections, despite repeatedly proposing tax increases and spending cuts. Merkel's policies led to Germany's economic growth and low unemployment through the 2007 to 2008 economic crisis, helping her country to navigate the changing landscape of European economics with the ongoing development of the European Union.

These successes have helped Merkel to govern without the

The first female chancellor of Germany, Angela Merkel is also the longest-serving head of government in the European Union.

opposition and turmoil that afflicts so many other nations and governments. In 2018, Merkel was the longest-serving head of government in Europe. In fact, in 2016, *Forbes* magazine placed her as number one on the list of "The 100 Most Powerful Women in the World." Merkel is best known for her fearless involvement in foreign affairs. Two examples include her strong push for diplomacy when Russia invaded Ukraine in 2014 and her generous opening of Germany's borders to take in tens of thousands of Syrian refugees at a time when most European countries refused to get involved in the Syrian crisis.

CHAPTER THREE

MADAME PRESIDENT

Presidents are elected as heads of state. Presidents often lead under a majority party in government, but not always, and not easily when they are up against a majority opposition. Depending on a country's laws, the president has the opportunity to serve any given number of terms. In the United States, the elected president has a maximum allowance of two terms of four years for a total of eight years.

Presidents tend to have more direct influence on governance than prime ministers, although policies must be introduced by party members or members of Congress in the case of the United States. For example, the president of the United States is the country's head of state and commander in chief of the armed forces. He or she has the power to write executive orders and veto bills.

Female presidents have not arrived at the highest office easily, and many start as activists in the ever-changing landscape of world politics.

Ellen Johnson Sirleaf

President of Liberia, Ellen Johnson Sirleaf, was one of the three winners of the 2011 Nobel Peace Prize and also the first woman to lead as president in an African nation. Sirleaf won the 2005 elections at the age of sixty-seven. The election process was closely watched by international observers to help curb corruption.

Sirleaf was a child bride. She endured domestic abuse in her marriage and was raising four children by her early twenties, when she left her children with family and traveled to the United States to pursue her college education at Harvard University. Sirleaf rose out of very difficult circumstances to better herself and her country.

Sirleaf's journey to serving in Liberia's government was not without severe turmoil. She was imprisoned, and her jailers threatened to bury

Winner of the 2011 Nobel Peace Prize, Ellen Johnson Sirleaf raises a hand to a cheering crowd in the capital city of Monrovia, Liberia, shortly before she was elected president.

her alive. In her autobiography, Sirleaf says that the prison guards moved her to a cell with all-male prisoners and forced her to watch as her fellow prisoners were executed one by one.

The women of Liberia were Sirleaf's number-one asset during the election. She recruited female supporters to seek out and register female voters in the most rural parts of the country. With these efforts, the voter turnout for Liberian women rose from 15 percent to 58 percent.

Shortly after her win in the 2005 election, she put on a pair of sneakers and played soccer against her opponent, whom she had just beaten. In this simple act, she demonstrated her understanding of the depth of healing Liberia needed following the end of a fourteen-year-long civil war. When the Ebola crisis struck, rapidly sweeping through the nation and taking the lives of thousands of her citizens, Sirleaf worked tirelessly to combat the epidemic. She called on the world's wealthiest countries to come to Liberia's aid.

Corazon Aquino

Corazon Aquino was born in 1933 and would grow up to succeed Ferdinand Marcos's twenty-year-long rule of the Philippines. Aquino was married to Benigno Simeon Ninoy Aquino Jr., President Marcos's main political opponent. When her husband was assassinated by government agents in 1983, Corazon was devastated.

WEALTH AND CORRUPTION

When Ferdinand Marcos and his wife, Imelda, famous for her extravagant taste and style, fled the Philippines for Hawaii in 1986, the military conceded the Philippines election to Corazon Aquino and her party. President Aquino kept her promises to release more than five hundred political prisoners and made the former ruler's palace a museum where citizens could witness the luxury that Marcos and his wife had lived in. Imelda Marcos had more than 1,000 pairs of shoes, 888 handbags, 71 pairs of sunglasses, and numerous priceless pieces of art. Although former president Marcos passed away in 1989 in Hawaii, Imelda returned to the Philippines in 1991 and was elected to the House of Representatives in 1995 and again in 2010. Imelda Marcos was accused, tried, and absolved of many charges regarding the dishonestly obtained wealth of the Marcos family, much of which has been seized by the Philippine government. In 2016, the government allowed much of the former first lady's jewelry to be sold at auction.

Aquino's reluctant entrance into politics moved forward only after a petition for her to run against Marcos after her husband's murder was signed by more than a million people in the Philippines. In 1986, thousands of those same citizens came out on the streets wearing yellow, Corazon's party's color.

The newly declared president of the Philippines, Corazon Aquino, reviewed her troops at a parade in January 1986.

This event is remembered as the "bloodless revolution" that returned the country to democracy. However, Marcos's supporters threatened lives at polling stations, tearing up ballots that voted against Marcos, and more than thirty people were killed trying to cast their votes.

When the election was over, both sides claimed they had won, but Aquino had the support of many world leaders who wanted Marcos to step down. Thousands of Aquino's supporters came to the streets to show their support. In fact, for four days straight, citizens stood up to and knelt before military tanks and gave soldiers flowers. The peaceful resistance worked. In 1986, Aquino became the first female president of the Philippines, while Marcos fled to Hawaii and lived in exile until the end of his life in 1989. Her presidency lasted until 1992, and Aquino had much work to do picking up the pieces of a country in which poverty and corruption were rampant. With the help of the

On February 7, 2010, Laura Chinchilla was elected president of Costa Rica, the first woman to hold that position and the fifth female president in Latin America.

US government, Aquino made some important changes. She wrote a new constitution that incorporated a division of power and checks and balances, like in the US Constitution. In 1992, in a peaceful transition of power, Aquino declined to run again and instead backed her former minister of defense, Fidel Ramos.

Laura Miranda Chinchilla

Laura Miranda Chinchilla was born in 1959. She was elected president of Costa Rica in 2010. Before her presidency, Chinchilla held jobs as a consultant for international agencies in Latin America and Africa. As a member of the National Liberation Party, she served two two-year terms as deputy minister of public security and minister of public security. In 2002, she served on the Legislative Assembly. Her legislative efforts focused on combating organized crime, public corruption, domestic violence, and crimes involving children. Chinchilla is well known for writing and speaking about human rights. She also advocated for free-trade agreements with various global trading partners.

In 2006, Chinchilla was elected vice president under President Óscar Arias Sánchez. Arias chose Chinchilla as his successor, and she became Costa Rica's first female president, winning forty-seven percent of the vote in 2010. Her four-year term was clouded by conflict with Nicaragua over a coastal river that bordered both countries, but she reached out to the International Court of Justice, and when they ruled for both sides to back down, peace was restored to Costa Rica.

Cristina Fernández de Kirchner

Cristina Fernández de Kirchner was the president of Argentina from 2007 until 2015. She was elected by a landslide margin to become Argentina's first female president and also the first wife to succeed her husband as president. A charismatic speaker, Kirchner was popular among the rural poor and suburban working class. She provided governmental stability by keeping over half of the ministers from the preceding government.

Born in La Plata, Fernández studied law at the National University of La Plata, where she met Néstor Kirchner, whom she married in 1975. Active since the 1970s in the Peronist Justicialist Party, she was

Former president Cristina Kirchner won a seat in Argentina's Senate on October 22, 2017. Despite scandals including corruption charges, she remained a popular president.

elected to the Santa Cruz provincial legislature in 1989. She was elected to the Senate in 1995 and 2001. Her husband was elected president in 2003. Fernández served as an itinerant ambassador for her husband's government.

President Fernández de Kirchner served as president from 2007 until 2015 and faced both seasons of popularity and opposition. She made headway on welfare, education, and health care, but the national debt had grown with her social programs by the time she handed off the baton to the next administration in 2015. However, Kirchner's presidency brought more positive changes than problems. She strengthened Argentina's trading partnership with Brazil, established new markets in China, and invested in social projects, such as cash payments to poor mothers. Argentina's unemployment rate fell to 7.3 percent, its lowest level in twenty years. Kirchner has been a leader of change and a champion of women.

Dilma Rousseff

Dilma Rousseff was president of Brazil from 2010 until 2016. Rousseff was born in 1947, the daughter of a Bulgarian immigrant lawyer and a Brazilian teacher. She studied to be an economist. A young opponent of Brazil's military dictatorship, Rousseff joined an oppositional guerrilla group in the 1960s. In 1970, she was captured,

Dilma Rousseff was the first female president of Brazil. She was also the first democratically elected female president in the world to be impeached and removed from office.

imprisoned, and tortured for nearly three years for her opposition to the military.

Rousseff became involved in local and state politics in 1986, and in 2000 she became a member of the Worker's Party. Beginning in 2003, she served in President Luiz Inácio Lula da Silva's cabinet as energy minister for two years. She served as his chief of staff from 2005 until 2010. An accusation of corruption nearly ruined her political career in 2009, but she survived the charges and became the

Worker's Party's presidential candidate in 2010. With President da Silva's support, she won the election.

During her presidency, Rousseff's opponents petitioned to impeach her thirty-seven times. In 2014, President Rousseff was reelected, her second win after a runoff election, but she never completed her second term. Corruption, inflation, and recession clouded her second term. In 2016, legislators voted to impeach her, accusing her of skewing the actual size of the government deficit and running a crime syndicate involving Petrobras, an oil company that President Rousseff was the chairperson of between 2003 and 2010. The criminal investigation into the matter became known as Operation Car Wash. She was removed from office in 2016 by a 61 to 20 vote in favor of her impeachment. Vice President Michel Temer stepped in as interim president of Brazil.

CHAPTER FOUR

WOMEN'S FIRSTS

It takes bravery and determination for women to enter politics. It is often a significant accomplishment for women to take on political endeavors, even if they don't succeed. For the most part, the world has been led by men. But things are changing, and women are running for and being elected to political offices women have never occupied before. Many of the female leaders discussed in previous chapters were the first to hold their positions of leadership. Many women have followed in their footsteps.

Many women of diverse ethnicities and sexual orientations have been elected to governmental offices in the United States, and as pioneers in their cities, states, and country, they are the women who have laid a foundation for lasting changes to American politics. According to statistics reported on the website of the Center for American

Women and Politics (CAWP), close to three hundred women have been elected to the US House of Representatives and close to 22 percent have been women of color. These women bring diversity to a political scene traditionally dominated by white men.

Jeannette Rankin

Elected in 1916, Jeannette Rankin was the first congresswoman in US history. At the time, only some states, including her home state of Montana, had women's suffrage. As a member of the House of Representatives, she supported women's suffrage and other women's issues. She voted in favor of the Nineteenth Amendment to grant women the right to vote in all fifty states. The Nineteenth Amendment was ratified in 1920.

Rankin ran for the Senate in 1918 as an independent after losing the Republican primary. She won a second term in the House in 1940. As a strong pacifist, she was the only member of Congress to vote against the declaration of war against Japan in 1941, which brought the United States into World War II following the attack on Pearl Harbor. The furor over her vote led her to decide against running for reelection. She had also opposed US involvement in World War I and voted against the declaration of war on Germany in 1917.

After moving to Georgia, Rankin became active in the Women's International League for Peace and Freedom and the National Consumer's League, and

NATIVE AMERICANS

Though women gained the right to vote with the passage of the Nineteenth Amendment in 1920, that still didn't mean that all women had the right to vote. Native Americans were granted suffrage in 1924. However, voting requirements, such as giving up their reservation homes, paying poll taxes, and being able to read and write, continued to limit the participation of Native Americans in elections.

Born in 1882, Cora Reynolds Anderson, a Native American woman, was the first woman elected to the Michigan House of Representatives. She served one term from 1925 until 1926. Anderson concentrated on public welfare issues, while also chairing the Industrial Home for Girls Committee. Her interest in public health issues focused on alcoholism and tuberculosis, which plagued Indian reservations at the time.

she founded the Georgia Peace Society. With her new position, she traveled the world as an advocate for peace and nonviolent resolutions to conflicts.

Patsy Takemoto Mink

Patsy Takemoto Mink became the first woman of color elected to the US House of Representatives when she won an election in Hawaii and began serving in

1965. A third-generation Japanese American, Mink grew up during a time of hostility toward Japanese Americans in the United States. After the Japanese military attacked Pearl Harbor in 1941, many people with Japanese heritage were not trusted and were subjected to mistreatment in the United States. Despite this unfavorable political climate, Mink was ambitious and steadfastly pursued her goals. After failing to get into medical school, she went to law school and graduated from the University of Chicago Law School, where she met her future husband, John Mink. It was uncommon at the time for a person of Japanese descent to marry a white person, but Patsy and John Mink were not deterred by this.

Mink began her political career as a member of the Hawaii Territorial Legislature in 1956, three years before Hawaii became the fiftieth state. She went on to serve in the US Congress from 1965 until 1977. She served for a second stretch beginning with her election in 1990 until her death in 2002. She remained steadfast in her beliefs and her platform as she worked hard for civil rights, women's rights, economic justice, and democratic integrity throughout her career. Mink was the primary author and advocate for Title IX, a law mandating that males and females receive equal treatment and funding in all programs related to education all the way to the college level. In 2014, President Barack Obama posthumously awarded Mink the Presidential Medal of Freedom.

The first woman of Japanese descent and the only woman to be elected to the 89th Congress, Patsy Mink created a homemade nameplate for the door of her new office.

Shirley Chisholm

Shirley Chisholm, a New York Democrat, became the first black woman to serve in Congress when she was elected in 1968. Her service in Congress began the following year, in 1969, and she served for a total of fourteen years. Chisholm was also the first black woman to run for president with a major party. Standing up to her peers in government, Chisholm announced her candidacy in 1972. Neither the candidate solely of black America nor solely of women, she represented both her race and her gender.

After the 1972 election, Chisholm said, "I ran because someone had to do it first. . . . I ran because most people thought the country was not ready for a black candidate, not ready for a woman candidate." Having run in the hope that her candidacy would help to reform the political situation in the United States, Chisholm continued to work in politics by campaigning for Jesse Jackson in 1984 and 1988 and by cofounding the National Political Congress of Black Women to give voice to black women's needs and concerns.

Carol Moseley Braun

In 1992, Carol Moseley Braun of Illinois was elected as the first black female senator in the United States. Having previously served in politics at the state and local levels, Braun was no stranger to government. During her six years in office, Braun fought hard for

Running her campaign on the principles of integrity and unity, Shirley Chisholm ran for president in the 1972 election and become the first African American female candidate for president of the United States as a member of a major party.

better schools, economic equality, and improvements to Social Security. But her time in the Senate was not without turmoil and controversy. She faced criticisms of her campaign spending, meeting with the Nigerian president, and the harassment charges pressed against her fiancé and campaign manager, Kgosie Matthews.

In 1998, Braun lost the election to the Senate but continued in politics as the American ambassador to New Zealand and Samoa. In 2003, Braun announced that she would run for the Democratic nomination for president, but in 2004 she dropped out of the running and endorsed Howard Dean instead. Braun is remembered for her perseverance on many issues, including opposing Congress's plan to tax mammograms, an important issue affecting women and the prevention of breast cancer.

Three-term Democratic senator Carol Moseley Braun speaks up for gay rights at a Human Rights Campaign event in Washington, D.C.

Sandra Day O'Connor

Born in 1930, Sandra Day O'Connor was the first female US Supreme Court justice. A graduate of Stanford Law School, O'Connor returned to practice in her home state of Arizona, where she was a state assistant attorney general for four years starting in 1965 and served as a Republican state senator from 1969 until 1974. In 1974, O'Connor was appointed a state judge and made it to the Arizona Court of Appeals in 1979. In 1981, President Reagan nominated her to the US Supreme Court. She was unanimously confirmed by the Senate, becoming the first female justice on the country's highest court.

O'Connor was the deciding vote in several critical cases during the 1990s, and she had a reputation for tackling issues on a case-by-case basis rather than relying on a political belief system. She finished her term as Supreme Court judge as a strong upholder of the Constitution. After leaving the court, O'Connor served on the Iraq Study Group, which was assembled in 2006 to advise the US government on the war in Iraq. In 2009, she founded iCivics, a nonprofit video game–based program that teaches middle school and high school students about American democracy. More than five million students used the program in 2016. In 2009, President Obama awarded her the Presidential Medal of Freedom.

Sandra Day O'Connor stands outside the US Supreme Court building on September 25, 1981, the day she was sworn in as the first female US Supreme Court justice.

Condoleezza Rice

Condoleezza Rice was born in 1954. She became the first female national security adviser in 2001 and the first African American woman to be secretary of state in 2005. (Madeleine Albright had been the first

DRESS FOR SUCCESS

The dress code for women in politics has changed over the years. In 1969, Charlotte T. Reid, a Republican representative from Illinois, was the first woman to wear pants on the House floor. She wore a black, wool pantsuit with bell bottoms. At the time, dresses and skirts were widely accepted as the unofficial dress code for women. Although wearing pants was discouraged, women continued to show up on Capitol Hill in pants. In 1993, Senators Barbara Mikulski, Nancy Kassebaum, and Carol Moseley Braun were the first women to wear pants on the Senate floor. After Illinois senator Moseley Braun repeatedly wore pants to work, Senate sergeant-at-arms Martha Pope circulated a memo updating the dress code to include "coordinated pantsuits." In 2017, more than thirty female representatives from both houses came to work on "Sleeveless Friday" wearing sleeveless dresses and tops to oppose the rule that women couldn't show their arms in Congress. As a result, Paul Ryan pledged to update the dress code for women in Congress, giving them more autonomy and variety in their attire.

female secretary of state, serving from 1997 until 2001. Rice's predecessor as secretary of state, Colin Powell, had been the first African American to hold the position.) Rice's areas of expertise were Russian and Eastern European studies. Before and after her positions in the federal government, she was a faculty member at Stanford University.

From 1989 until 1991, Rice advised President George H. W. Bush on Soviet and Eastern European affairs on his National Security Council. Rice continued to advise his son George W. Bush on foreign policy during the 2000 election, and in 2001 he selected her as his national security adviser. During her years as national security adviser, Rice was an assertive voice on American foreign policy, a champion of US military power, and a supporter of the invasion of Iraq.

Nancy Pelosi

A Democrat from California, Nancy Pelosi has served in the House of Representatives since 1987. She was the first woman to serve as Speaker of the House of Representatives, a position she held from 2007 until 2011.

Pelosi's years in Congress earned her a reputation as a consistent advocate for gay rights, abortion access, health care for the poor, and human rights. When Iraqi president Saddam Hussein invaded Kuwait in 1991, Pelosi voted against military intervention by the United States.

The first female Speaker of the House, Nancy Pelosi, celebrates her new position surrounded by the children and grandchildren of various members of the House.

In October 2001, she was elected the Democratic Party whip, making her the party's second in command. The party whip is responsible for teaming up with party members and forming a plan to get laws passed that the party supports. Pelosi was elected House minority leader in 2002. She was the first woman in the history of the US Congress to secure the top post in a major political party. But her rise in the ranks wasn't over yet.

After the 2006 election, Pelosi was chosen as the first female Speaker of the House of Representatives after the Democratic Party took the majority in Congress. Pelosi became known for her avid support of health care reform. In the 2010 elections, the Republican Party took control of Congress. In

2018, Pelosi served as minority leader of the House of Representatives.

Ileana Ros-Lehtinen

Ileana Ros-Lehtinen, a Florida Republican, became the first Latina woman and first Cuban American to be elected to Congress. Ros-Lehtinen was elected to the Florida State House of Representatives in 1982 and to the Florida Senate in 1986. She was the first Latina woman to serve in either body. Ros-Lehtinen sponsored the legislation for the Florida Prepaid College Program, the largest prepaid college tuition program in the nation. This opened up a door for many students who otherwise wouldn't have the opportunity to get a college education.

Ros-Lehtinen was elected to the US House of Representatives in 1989. She has been a strong supporter of reducing taxes and government spending and advocates for a balanced budget and tax incentives for small businesses and middle-class families. She also supports Head Start, a federal government childhood development and education program for the advancement of children ages three and four, and the Violence Against Women Act. She is an important advocate for veterans and is particularly vocal about women's contributions to the US armed forces. She is also a firm advocate for human rights and fighting terrorism globally.

Ileana Ros-Lehtinen, pictured on Capitol Hill in 1989 with her husband and two children, was the first Latina woman elected to Congress and as a Florida state senator.

Hillary Rodham Clinton

Hillary Rodham Clinton was the first female candidate to be nominated for president by one of the major political parties in the United States. She was not, however, the first woman to run for president. Almost fifty years before women gained the right to vote nationwide, Victoria Woodhull ran for president as the nominee of the Equal Rights Party in 1872.

Born in 1947, Clinton was interested in and active in politics long before she met her husband, Bill. After Bill Clinton was elected president in 1992, Clinton received her first official government role as chair of the Task Force on National Health Care Reform. Under the shadow of her husband's impeachment in 1998, Clinton did not lay down her

On the campaign trail, Hillary Clinton shares her vision for America's future at the Apollo Theater in New York City.

political dreams. She was elected to the US Senate, representing New York, in 2000 and was reelected in 2006. In 2008, she ran for president but narrowly lost the Democratic Party nomination to Barack Obama. After Obama was elected, she served as the secretary of state during his first term (from 2009 until 2013). Clinton dealt with many foreign policy challenges, including an attack on the American embassy in Benghazi, Libya, in which several Americans were killed. This incident followed her into the 2016 presidential race.

Clinton won the Democratic nomination for president in 2016, but her campaign was dogged, and perhaps ultimately doomed, by relentless coverage of her use of a private email server during her tenure as secretary of state. Although Donald Trump, the Republican candidate, won the 2016 election by triumphing in the Electoral College, Clinton won the popular vote by more than three million votes. Her journey in politics has inspired people all over the world. Clinton is known for her stand against gun violence and her advocacy for immigration and health care reform. She is a powerful voice in US politics.

Michelle Obama

Michelle Obama became the first African American First Lady of the United States when her husband, Barack Obama, was elected president in 2008. She

FIRST LADIES OF THE UNITED STATES

First Ladies of the United States are remembered for more than the gowns they wore to their husbands' inaugural balls. Abigail Fillmore, whose husband, Millard, was president from 1850 until 1853, was a First Lady who loved books and championed learning. It was on her initiative that the White House library was established. First Lady Edith Wilson intervened when President Woodrow Wilson had a stroke in 1919, deciding which items were important enough to bring to the president's attention.

Eleanor Roosevelt has a long list of accomplishments associated with civil rights and women's rights. She resigned her membership in the Daughters of the American Revolution when the organization prevented the black opera singer Marian Anderson from performing at Constitution Hall in 1939. After her husband, Franklin, died in 1945, Eleanor Roosevelt was appointed as a delegate to the United Nations and was involved in the drafting and adoption of the Universal Declaration of Human Rights in 1948.

Jacqueline Kennedy spearheaded major renovations to the White House and then took the nation on a televised tour of the Kennedy family's household. Betty Ford was a vocal proponent of the Equal Rights Amendment, abortion rights, and breast cancer awareness. Rosalynn Carter was the first First Lady to sit in on the president's Cabinet meetings.

met Barack Obama while working at a law firm in Chicago soon after graduating from Harvard Law School. They married in 1992. The Obamas have two daughters, Malia and Sasha.

As First Lady, Michelle Obama focused on being a role model for women and an advocate for family health and armed services members and their families. She also stressed the importance of higher education, particularly for young women in places where cultural barriers prevent them from going to school. She initiated a program called Let's Move! to help combat childhood obesity. In 2011, she and Vice President Biden's wife, Dr. Jill Biden, started Joining Forces, an outreach program to increase opportunities and care for veterans and families with a member in active services. In 2015, Obama launched the Reach Higher initiative, a program designed to encourage teens to pursue college dreams. Obama's Let Girls Learn program was an initiative promoting education for girls worldwide.

As part of the Joining Forces initiative, First Lady Michelle Obama and Jill Biden meet with volunteers preparing food for family members of Wounded Warriors. The Wounded Warriors Project supports wounded service members and their families.

Working tirelessly and with poise and passion, Obama is an inspiration to girls and women across the world. She will be remembered for her simple yet profound words at the Democratic National Convention in 2016: "When they go low, we go high."

Sarah Palin

Sarah Palin's family moved to Alaska not long after she was born in 1964. She entered Alaskan local politics in 1992 and served two terms on the Wasilla City Council and two terms as mayor of her hometown, Wasilla, Alaska. Palin is a Republican and a social conservative. In 2002, Palin made an unsuccessful bid for the Republican nomination for lieutenant governor. She chaired the Alaska Oil and Gas Conservation Commission in 2003 and early 2004, but ethical conflicts led her to resign after serving less than a year.

In 2006, Palin became Alaska's first female governor. As governor of Alaska, Palin

Sarah Palin took the political world by surprise when she became the first woman to be on the Republican ballot for vice president in a presidential election.

supported state savings, education, and the Senior Benefits Program, which helps low-income elderly citizens of her state. She also stood up to big oil companies, signing legislation like ACES (Alaska Clear and Equitable Share), which protected oil producers when oil prices dropped while simultaneously looking out for Alaskan citizens.

Chosen in 2008 by Republican presidential candidate John McCain to be his running mate, Palin became the first woman to be nominated for the vice presidency by the Republican Party. (Geraldine Ferraro was the first woman nominated as vice president by a major political party. She was Democratic candidate Walter Mondale's running mate in 1984, when they lost to Ronald Reagan and George H. W. Bush.) The McCain-Palin ticket lost the election to Democrats Barack Obama and Joe Biden. Palin resigned as governor

LGBTQ+ POLITICIANS

In the early 1970s, only ten cities in the United States had laws that protected homosexual rights, including Ann Arbor, Michigan. In 1974, Kathy Kozachenko became the first openly gay person to be elected to a public office in the United States when she won a seat on the Ann Arbor City Council. A student at the University of Michigan, Kozachenko ran as a Human Rights Party candidate. Kozachenko was a forerunner to Harvey Milk, who was elected to the

San Francisco Board of Supervisors in 1977. Elaine Noble was the first openly lesbian congresswoman from Massachusetts and the first openly gay candidate elected to a state-level office. She was elected to the House of Representatives in 1975.

In 2006, Kim Coco Iwamoto became the first transgender official to win state office in Hawaii. She served on Hawaii's state Board of Education until

(continued on the next page)

When she was elected to Hawaii's Board of Education in 2006, Kim Coco Iwamoto was the highest-elected transgender official in the United States.

(continued from the previous page)

2011. Iwamoto focused on issues of homelessness, the arts, and bullying. Kate Brown was elected the first openly bisexual governor in the country in 2015. As Oregon's thirty-eighth governor, Brown has worked hard on the issues of education, climate change, and affordable health care.

Tammy Baldwin was the first woman elected to represent Wisconsin in Congress. In 1998, Baldwin ran and won her first national election, making her the first openly gay person to take a seat in the US House of Representatives, where she represented Wisconsin for seven terms. In 2012, Baldwin won the Senate race and became the first openly gay person in US history elected as a senator.

in 2009, before the end of her term. After that, she supported Tea Party candidates, wrote two books, and hosted a reality show about living in Alaska.

Nikki Haley

Nimrata "Nikki" Randhawa Haley is a first-generation Indian American who was born in South Carolina in 1972. Haley won a seat in the South Carolina House of Representatives in 2004, and she was reelected in 2006 and 2008. A Republican, she has been an education advocate, fought for tax reform, including the elimination of small business income tax, and pushed for stricter immigration laws. She was elected governor of South Carolina in November 2010.

She is the first female governor in South Carolina's history and the second Indian American governor in the history of the United States, after Bobby Jindal of Louisiana. Although she spoke up against Donald Trump on different issues, including his proposed Muslim ban, she accepted his nomination to become the US ambassador to the United Nations in 2017.

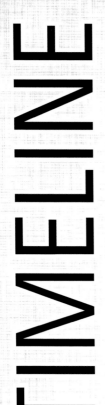

TIMELINE

1473 BCE Hatshepsut begins ruling as pharaoh of Egypt.

1762 Catherine the Great begins her rule as empress of Russia.

1869 Wyoming, at the time still a territory, becomes the first state or territory of the United States to give women the right to vote.

1872 Victoria Woodhull becomes the first woman to run for president of the United States.

1916 Jeannette Rankin becomes the first woman elected to the US Congress.

1920 The Nineteenth Amendment to the US Constitution is ratified, giving women the right to vote in all states.

1952 Elizabeth II becomes queen of the United Kingdom and Northern Ireland.

1964 Patsy Takemoto Mink is elected, becoming the first woman of color in the US House of Representatives.

1966 Indira Gandhi is elected as prime minister of India for four nonconsecutive terms.

1974 Kathy Kozachenko is elected, becoming the first openly gay elected official in American politics, serving on the Ann Arbor City Council.

1981 Sandra Day O'Connor is appointed and confirmed as the first female justice of the US Supreme Court.

1989 Ileana Ros-Lehtinen is elected to the House of Representatives, becoming the first Latina woman to serve in Congress.

1997 Princess Diana is killed in a car accident in France.

2005 Ellen Johnson Sirleaf is elected the president of Liberia, becoming the first elected female head of state in Africa.

2005 Angela Merkel becomes the first female chancellor of Germany.

2008 Michelle Obama becomes the first African American First Lady of the United States when her husband, Barack, is elected president.

2016 Hillary Rodham Clinton becomes the first woman nominated as a major party's presidential candidate in the United States.

GLOSSARY

activist A person who stands up for a political issue.

advocate To champion, speak up for, and rally support on an issue being discussed in government.

ambassador A person responsible for communication and peaceful relations between one nation and another.

assassination The murder of a political figure.

attorney general A Cabinet position appointed by the US president; the person is the head of the US Department of Justice and a primary legal adviser to the government.

chancellor The title given to the head of state in Germany. It is similar to a prime minister, elected every four years by the members of the Bundestag (German parliament).

coup The overthrow of a governing body.

dictatorship A form of government in which a country is ruled by one person.

domestic Refers to issues and government policies in the home country, not abroad.

exile The state of being expelled from one's country.

impeachment The legal process of removing a high government official from office.

inauguration The formal admission of someone to political office.

monarch A sovereign head of state, usually a king, queen, or emperor.

nomination The proposal that someone run for political office.

pacifist Someone who is opposed to war.

pharaoh The name given to the ruler of Egypt before the Roman Empire conquered Egypt in 30 BCE.

political party A group of voters organized to support certain public policies, with the goal of electing officials who will try to carry out those policies.

posthumous After death.

refugees People who flee their homes and countries to escape danger or persecution.

secretary of state The person who carries out the president's foreign policies through the State Department, including the Foreign Service, Civil Service, and US Agency for International Development.

suffrage The right to vote in political elections.

term The period one is assigned to political office.

FOR MORE INFORMATION

Canadian Museum of History
100 Laurier Street
Gatineau, QC
K1A 0M8
Canada
(800) 555-5621
Website: http://www.historymuseum.ca/cmc
    /exhibitions/tresors/treasure/283eng.shtml
Twitter and Facebook: @CanMusHistory
Instagram: @canmushistory
The Canadian Museum of History is the largest
    museum in Canada and its mission is to reflect
    the events, people, stories, and objects that
    exemplify Canada's history.

Center for American Women and Politics (CAWP)
191 Ryders Lane
New Brunswick, NJ 08901-8557
(848) 932-9384
Website: http://www.cawp.rutgers.edu
Twitter: @CAWP_RU
Facebook: @womenandpolitics
YouTube: @CAWPvideos
The Center for American Women and Politics (CAWP)
    at Rutgers University in New Jersey is committed
    to scholarly research, updated data, and sharing

knowledge about American women and their roles in politics and government.

Equal Voice
99 - 1500 Bank Street
Suite 603, Ottawa ON
K1H 1B8
Canada
(613) 236-0302
Email: info@equalvoice.ca
Website: https://www.equalvoice.ca/facts.cfm
Twitter @EqualVoiceCA
Equal Voice is dedicated to women in Canadian politics, regardless of party affiliation.

League of Women in Government (LWG)
1901 E. 4th Street, Suite 100
Santa Ana, CA 92705
(805) 252-6468
Website: http://leagueofwomeningovernment.org
Email: info@leagueofwomeningovernment.org
Twitter and Facebook: @WomenLeadingGov
Instagram: @leagueofwomeningovernment
The League of Women in Government (LWG) serves as the umbrella organization to support local and statewide organizations that advance women in local government leadership.

Library of Congress
101 Independence Avenue SE
Washington, DC 20540

(202) 707-5000
Website: https://www.loc.gov
Twitter and Instagram: @librarycongress
Facebook and YouTube: @libraryofcongress
The Library of Congress is the largest library in the
    world and the main research source for the US
    government.

She Should Run
718 7th Street NW, 2nd Floor
Washington, DC 20001
 (202) 796-8396
Website: http://www.sheshouldrun.org
Email: info@sheshouldrun.org
Twitter, Facebook, and Instagram: @sheshouldrun
YouTube: @She Should Run
She Should Run is an organization that provides a
    starting place and network for female leaders
    considering running for office in the future.

United Nations
405 East 42nd Street
New York, NY 10017
(212) 963-9999
Website: http://www.un.org/en/index.html
Twitter: @un
Facebook, YouTube, and Instagram: @unitednations
The United Nations is a group of nations that
    collectively strive to maintain international
    peace and security, protect human rights,
    deliver humanitarian aid, promote sustainable

development, and uphold international law.

Women Suffrage and Beyond
University of British Columbia
Vancouver, BC
Canada
Website: http://womensuffrage.org
Email: submit@womensuffrage.org
Twitter: @WomenSuffrage
Facebook: @WomenSuffrageAndBeyond
Women Suffrage and Beyond is an electronic,
    academic journal based out of the University
    of British Columbia that researches, reports,
    and cites news stories that reflect the state of
    women's suffrage globally.

FOR FURTHER READING

Brower, Kate Andersen. *First Women: The Grace and Power of America's Modern First Ladies*. New York, NY: HarperCollins, 2017.

Clinton, Hillary. *What Happened*. New York, NY: Simon & Schuster, 2017.

Cooper, Helene. *Madame President: The Extraordinary Journey of Ellen Johnson Sirleaf*. New York, NY: Simon and Schuster, 2017.

Dolan, Julie, Melissa M. Deckman, and Michele L. Swers. *Women and Politics: Paths to Power and Politics.* Lanham, MD: Rowman and Littlefield Publishers, 2017.

Henderson, Sarah L., and Alana S. Jeydel. *Women and Politics in a Global World*. Oxford, United Kingdom: Oxford University Press, 2013.

Linderman, Juliet. "A Look at Women's Advances over the Years in Congress." *PBS NewsHour,* November 4, 2017.

Moore, Charles. *Margaret Thatcher: The Authorized Biography, from Grantham to the Falklands*. New York, NY: Vintage Books, 2013.

Paxton, Pamela, and Melanie M. Hughes, eds. *Women, Politics, and Power: A Global Perspective.* Thousand Oaks, CA: CQ Press, 2016.

Popham, Peter. *The Lady and the Peacock: The Life of Aung San Suu Kyi.* New York, NY: The Experiment Publishing, 2012.

Schupack, Sara. *Indira Gandhi*. New Rochelle, NY:
   Benchmark Books, 2014.
Swain, Susan, and C-SPAN. *First Ladies: Presidential
   Historians on the Lives of 45 Iconic American
   Women*. New York, NY: Public Affairs, 2015.

BIBLIOGRAPHY

Ackerman, Ruthie. "Mother of a Nation: Liberia's President." *Christian Science Monitor,* January 2007, Vol. 99, Issue 32.

Alonzo, Vincent. "Under Glass." *Successful Meetings*, May 2002, Vol. 51, Issue 5.

Alter, Charlotte. "What We Can Learn from Nellie Tayloe Ross, America's First Female Governor." *Time.com*, November 2014. http://time .com/3555677/nellie-tayloe-ross.

Axelrod-Contrada, Joan. "Corazòn Aquino Yellow Rose of the Philippines." *Women Who Led Nations*. Minneapolis, MN: The Oliver Press, 1999.

Bennett, Joy T. "Liberia's President Ellen Johnson Sirleaf's remarkable life." *Ebony*, May 2009, Volume 64.

Black, Allida. "The First Ladies of the United States of America." White House Historical Association, 2009.

Burt, Jan. *Sonia Gandhi*. Great Neck, NY: Great Neck Publishing, 2006.

Clinton, Hillary. *Hard Choices*. New York, NY: Simon & Schuster, 1994.

CNN Library. "Carol Moseley Braun Fast Facts." August 2, 2017. https://www.cnn.com /2013/07/26/us/carol-moseley-braun-fast -facts/index.html.

CNN Library. "Queen Elizabeth II Fast Facts." April 23, 2017. http://www.cnn.com/2012/12/17 /world/europe/queen-elizabeth-ii—fast-facts /index.html.

Deerwester, Jayme. "Timeline: Princess Diana's Life and the Events That Made Her Who She Was." *USA Today*, August 23, 2017. https://www.usatoday.com/story/life/people/2017/08/23/timeline-princess-dianas-life/508263001.

Doksone, Thanyarat. "Thai ex-PM Starts Trial for Role in Rice Subsidy Scheme." *Jakarta Post*, May 19, 2015. http://www.thejakartapost.com/news/2015/05/19/thai-ex-pm-starts-trial-role-rice-subsidy-scheme.html.

Dunn, Hannah-Louise. "Late Princess Diana's compassion extended to blacks worldwide." *Jet*, September 1997, Vol. 92, Issue 18.

Flanders, Stephen. "Political Parties." *The New Book of Knowledge®*. Grolier Online, July 25, 2007.

Greve, Joan. "LGBT America: By the Numbers." *Washington Week Fellow*, PBS, June 2016.

Her Majesty Queen Rania Al Abdullah. https://www.queenrania.jo/en/rania.

Hilleary, Cecily. "Why Aren't More Native Americans Members of the US Congress?" VOANews, April 7, 2017.

Keene, Ann T. "Mink, Patsy." American National Biography. http://www.anb.org/articles/07/07-00812.html.

Kelly, Martin. "The 10 Most Influential First Ladies." Thoughtco.com, September 7, 2017.

Lanser, Amanda. *Women in Politics and Government*. Minniapolis, MN: Abdo Publishing, 2017.

Lawson, Linda S. "Before dawn breaks." *Black*

Elegance, November, 1998, Issue 115.

Lewis, Danny. "Victoria Woodhull Ran for President Before Women Had the Right to Vote." *Smithsonian Magazine*, May 2016. http://www .smithsonianmag.com/smart-news/victoria -woodhull-ran-for-president-before-women-had-the -right-to-vote.

LGBT History Month. "Kathy Kozachenko." https:// lgbthistorymonth.com/kathy -kozachenko?tab=biography.

Lockwood, Siorna. "Inside Tucson Business Five Arizona women who made a difference." *Inside Tucson Business*, April 2006, Vol. 15.

Martin, J., and Mart Martin. *The Almanac of Women and Minorities in World Politics.* Boulder, CO: Westview Press, 2000.

Martin, Patricia. *Golda Meir*. New York, NY: Great Neck Publishing, 2005.

Martin, Patricia. *Indira Gandhi*. New York, NY: Great Neck Publishing, 2017.

Mathisen, Ralph W. "Galla Placidia." An Online Encyclopedia of Roman Emperors, June 1, 1999. https://www.roman-emperors.org/galla.htm.

McNamara, Alix, with Caroline Howard. "The 100 Most Powerful Women in the World." *Forbes*, June 16, 2016.

Morin, Isobel V. *Women of the U.S. Congress*. Minneapolis, MN: Oliver Press, 1994.

Nietzsche, Frederick. *The Twilight of Idols*. Indianapolis, IN: Hackett Publishing Company, 1997.

Norton, Elizabeth. "Women Rule." *Britain*, July/August 2015. Vol. 83, Issue 4.

Oregon.gov. "Governor Kate Brown: Moving Oregon Forward." http://www.oregon.gov/gov/Pages /index.aspx.

Patsy Takemoto Mink Education Foundation. http:// www.patsyminkfoundation.org.

Rigby, Claire. "Dilma Rousseff's rotten politics." *New Statesman*, April 2016, Vol. 145, Issue 5311.

Ronayne, Kathleen. "Nancy Pelosi Gets Shut Down by Young Immigrants over DACA Deal." *Time.com*, September 2017. http://time.com/4947508 /nancy-pelosi-dreamers-daca.

Ros-Lehtinen, Ileana. "Biography." Retrieved March 26, 2018. https://ros-lehtinen.house.gov/ about-me/full-biography.

Royal UK. "About Her Majesty the Queen." https:// www.royal.uk/her-majesty-the-queen.

Salisbury, Joyce E. *Rome's Christian Empress: Galla Placidia Rules at the Twilight of the Empire*. Baltimore, MD: Johns Hopkins University Press, 2015.

Samuelson, Kate. "Read Prime Minister Theresa May's Full Speech on the London Bridge Attack." *Time*, June 4, 2017.

Schons, Mary. "Women's Suffrage." *National Geographic*, January 2011.

Sirleaf, Ellen Johnson. *This Child Will Be Great: Memoir of a Remarkable Life by Africa's First Woman President*. New York, NY: HarperCollins, 2009.

Specia, Megan. "The Rohingya in Myanmar: How Years of Strife Grew into a Crisis." *New York Times*, September 2017.

Stewart, Dan. "Britain's Theresa May Says Brexit Shouldn't Take Effect Until 2021." *Time*, September 2017.

Stocker, Ed, Sara Miller Llana. "Cristina Fernandez de Kirchner, Argentina's comeback president?" *Christian Science Monitor,* October 2011.

Title IX. http://www.titleix.info.

Wade, Donna. "Senator Tammy Baldwin Is the Real Deal." *Lesbian News*, June 2013, Vol. 38, Issue 11.

Wilson, Elizabeth. "The Queen Who Would be King." *Smithsonian Magazine*, September 2006. https://www.smithsonianmag.com/history/the-queen-who-would-be-king-130328511.

Yourish, Karen, Larry Buchanan, and Adam Pearce. "Hillary Clinton Broke One Glass Ceiling. When Were Others Broken?" *New York Times*, July 25, 2016. https://www.nytimes.com/interactive/2016/07/25/us/politics/political-firsts.html.

INDEX

About the Author

Rajdeep Paulus studied English literature at Northwestern University. Paulus is the award-winning author of the *Swimming Through Clouds* trilogy of contemporary young adult novels. She became a writer after being inspired by her high school English teacher. When she's not writing, Paulus likes to kayak, play basketball, and dance like no one's watching. Paulus lives in New York with her Sunshine and four daughters.

Photo Credits